Khalil Gibran's

How I Became a Madman

Parables of Wisdom & Folly

A Derivative by
Beverly A. Potter

RONIN
Berkeley, CA

Khalil Gibran's

How I Became a Madman

Parables of Wisdom & Folly

A Derivative by
Beverly A. Potter

How I Became a Madman

Copyright 2018 by Ronin Publishing, Inc.

ISBN: 978-1-57951-256-9 Pbook

ISBN: 978157951-257-6 Ebook

Published by

Ronin Publishing, Inc.

PO Box 3436

Oakland, CA 94609

www.roninpub.com

Production:

    Deriviative creation: Beverly A. Potter.

    Cover Design: Brian Groppe.

    Book Design: Beverly A. Potter.

    Photos: Fotolia and Pixabay

Library of Congress Card Number: 2018939871

Manufactured in the United States by Lightning Source.

Distributed to the book trade by PGW/Ingram.

Acknowledgments

Thanks to Scotty Hardwig and Mark Schapiro for brainstorm-ming facets of *How I Became a Madman*; to Mike Mari-nacci for remembering the *Alice in Wonderland madness quote;* thanks to Project Gutenberg for gathering and making available public domain Works, thanks to PGW for their support and getting this little book to market, and thanks to you, Dear Reader, for taking it home with you.

"Have I gone mad? I'm afraid so.
You're entirely Bonkers.
But I will tell you a secret,
All the best people are."

—Lewis Carroll
Alice in Wonderland

The brown text denotes the original Work of Kahlil Gibran;
the black text is material created for this derivitive.

Table of Contents

Table of Contents continued:

Introduction

Known for his evocative and influential book, *The Prophet*, Lebanese-born poet and artist Kahlil Gibran is the third best-selling poet of all time, behind Shakespeare and Lao Tzu. Gibran's most original work, *The Madman: His Parables and Poems,* delineates madness—not as a formal mental illness, but rather as an expression of the existential angst that results from the separation of the individual from society. Gibran contrasts the 'normal' individual who conforms to societal roles defined by legal, class and behavioral constraints with one who sees through hypocrisy and power plays, and is often judged by others as deceived or treacherous—the 'madman'. While the world classifies him as mad, he is the wise one.

How I Became a Madman consists of Gibran's thirty-four sketches, vignettes, and parables. Interspersed throughout are reflections from leading thinkers and philosophers on the role of 'the madman' in society, and further reflections on related themes of the 'outsider'.

Khalil Gibran

Gibran shows that we wear masks to get along in a society that demands conformity, an act of collective absorption into the dominant model of behavior and thought. When we look beneath the masks of daily life, we find greed, pride, sloth, ambition, vanity. Such people do not see anything wrong with the ways of the world.

Whereas to act without a mask, to think and speak and behave without the veil of illusion is to be 'mad'. While being mask-less unburdens us, it carries risk of loneliness and misunderstanding as we become estranged from others. The madman goes unnoticed. But in madness there is wisdom.

How I Became a Madman is a heart-felt critique of the ways in which hypocrisy, wealth, arrogance and power are poised against the individual. The madman has learned to disengage, to keep a distance. Nevertheless, he relates to others with compassion and kindness.

How I Became a Madman is a uniquely synergetic portrait of creative figures grappling with the conundrums of existence from the edges of society. It reflects the influence of Gibran's origins in the Levant, as his Arabic and Eastern literary structure and reflective lyricism reveals.

—Beverly Potter

An exploration of madness—the existential angst of melancholy and misfortune that separates the individual from society, not a formal mental illness.

1

Poet-Philosopher-Prophet

Gibran introduced a new style to Arab poets, who generally prided themselves on using words that had to be looked up in a dictionary, with his use of short and simple words in his early poetry. His first writings express dismay over the poor and oppressive conditions in his homeland, often urging his countrymen to revolt against the Turks. Gibran's writings during this period reflect his desire to revolt against the social, the religious, and the literary forms of the day.

Gibran's best works are considered to be those written between 1918 and his death in 1931. This was his second literary period, during which he wrote in English. His

Khalil Gibran

themes evolved from revolt to contentment and peace. He wrote few poems during this period. The poems he did compose reflect the same topics as his prose: the power of universal love, nature, and the essential goodness of humanity. Gibran's English prose consists of moral fables, aphorisms, fragments of conversation, and parables.

There are similarities between Gibran's writings of the two periods. In the first he frequently based his characters and setting on himself and his homeland. *The Broken Wings*, set in

Lebanon, for example, is believed to be autobiographical. Similarly, in *The Prophet*, Almustafa, the young prophet is thought to be Gibran. The return to the "isle of his birth" is seen as Gibran's desire to return to Lebanon.

During the second phase, Gibran considered himself a poet-philosopher-prophet. This character combination was common in Arabic literary circles, but did not have a counterpart in the American literature. In the West philosophers were supposed to think more deeply and objectively than other people, analyzing facts and events. By contrast, Gibran does not much conform to the Western concept of what a philosopher does.

Themes of mysticism, simplicity, imagery, metrical beauty, wisdom, and lofty visions are common in Gibran's work. Central to his writings are eternal questions, like "Where did humankind come from and where is it going?" and "What is humankind's purpose?" He frequently deals with the need to know oneself in human relationships and questions about life and death. Gibran's writings reflect his beliefs that humans are social beings who must coexist and life is a mixture of joy and suffering, and that we are responsible for our destiny. Other favorite themes include the difficulties women endure, the need for truth over law, the notion of love as a unifying force in nature, the importance of work, and the possibility of reincarnation return to finish the work left undone.

Gibran's writings spark our imagination. It may be the multiple messages conveyed within the same work, the similes or metaphors drawn from nature, or the various moods created by simple words.

Gibran's style has two characteristic keys. First, there is parallelism, repetition, and refrain. The second is a rhythm often found in biblical and other sacred writings. While these qualities are not common in American literature, they greatly influenced Arabic literature, which may be one reason why Gibran's writings have never received much attention from American literary scholars.

2

What is a Parable?

The word 'parable' comes from the Greek word *parabole*, which means *"to throw alongside"*. Parables are stories that use everyday objects to teach deeper philosophical truths most people would not grasp otherwise.

A parable does not necessarily hide the lesson; rather, it teaches in such a way that it can be grasped better by those who are opened to its understanding. A parable is beyond logic, metaphor, allegory, or abstract reasoning; it stimulates the interest to open our eyes and ears to engage our mind to seek truth, as a means of grasping eternal lessons. Parables cause us to think beyond the simple solution. It is a tool to challenge us to grow deeper and allow for questions.

A parable doesn't usually make sense the first time you hear it because it is a riddle written as a story that compares two things, one of which we understand and the other we're trying to understand. Parables include metaphors, similes and word-pictures. A good parable makes us visualize the meaning of the hidden subject,

Jesus used parables to explain divine truths.

> Parables help us see beyond the obvious into a deeper meaning. If you think you know what the parable means at first reading, chances are you missed the point. to understand it better because of the connection to the things we already know about and understand.

Jesus frequently used parables as a means of illustrating profound, divine truths. Stories such as His are easily remembered, the characters bold, and the symbolism rich in meaning. Jesus drew his stories from ordinary life. Parables do not define things precisely, but use comparisons to point us in the direction of understanding. The meaning of parables is never obvious, and indeed, the purpose of parables is not to settle issues, but to challenge us to think more deeply about the issues.

If you think you know what the parable means at first reading, chances are you missed the point. This is because parables are not as clear as you might expect. The truth is hidden by our pride, arrogance, preoccupation, hurts, expectations, and the tyranny of what we think is important.

There is often some doubt about the exact point of the parable, and the result is that we wonder why the story is so strange or unsettling—"Hey, that's not supposed to happen that way!"—causing us to think more deeply about its meaning. That is the goal—parables raise more questions than answers. Parables help us see beyond the obvious into a deeper meaning.

3

How I Became A Madman

You ask me how I became a madman. It happened thus: One day, long before many gods were born, I woke from a deep sleep and found all my masks were stolen— the seven masks I have fashioned and worn in seven lives— I ran maskless through the crowded streets shouting, "Thieves, thieves, the cursed thieves." Men and women laughed at me and some ran to their houses in fear of me.

And when I reached the market place, a youth standing on a house-top cried, "He is a madman." I looked up to behold him; the sun kissed my own naked face for the first time. For the first time the sun kissed my own naked face and my soul was inflamed with love for the sun, and I wanted my masks no more.

And as if in a trance I cried, "Blessed, blessed are the thieves who stole my masks." Thus I became a madman.

And I have found both freedom and safety in my madness; the freedom of loneliness and the safety from being understood, for those who understand us enslave something in us.

But let me not be too proud of my safety. Even a Thief in a jail is safe from another thief.

- - -

The madman may come to his view from having suffered a cruel fate or he may simply be too aware of the nature of things and too honest to ignore the truth of the mask or to dissemble his perception. Society classifies him as mad, but, in fact he is the wise one.

Gibran serenades the liberating madness of casting our masks aside. The normal person wears masks in order to function in society, to maintain self-identity in a world that corrodes the self and redefines it for its collective purpose. To act without a mask, to think and speak and behave without this veil of illusion, to cast political correctness aside, is to be mad.

To lose these masks, to be true to self and therefore true to nature and reality, is to be free. This freedom, taken against society, has its risk of loneliness and misunderstanding, but it safeguards intuition and self from the intolerant masses and their expectation of conformity, of mask-wearing.

> To act without a mask, to think and speak and behave without this veil of illusion, to cast PC aside, is to be MAD!

Outcast
*One who is cast out or rejected
by society.*

Castoff
*One who is no longer wanted;
abandoned or discarded.*

Pariah
*One who is not accepted by a
social group because of being not
liked, respected, or trusted.*

Reject
*One who is dismissed as failing to
meet standards or satisfy tastes.*

Untouchable
One who is of a low class.

Outsider
One who does not belong.

Offscouring
*One who is rejected and soured
off by society.*

Lonely
One who is without friends.

Castaway
*One who is stranded in an
isolated place.*

Forsaken
One who has been abandoned.

Excluded
*One who is denied access to a
place, group, or privilege.*

Vagabond
*One who wanders from place to
place without a home or job.*

Reprobate
One who is unprincipled.

Exile
*One who is barred from one's
native country.*

Outlaw
*One who has broken the law,
and is a fugitive.*

Derelict
One without a home or job.

Refugee
*One who forced to leave his
country to escape persecution.*

Friendless
One who is without friends.

Solitary
One who is a recluse or hermit.

Abandoned
One who has been cast off.

Alone
One with no one else present.

Wretched
*One who is unhappy and in an
unfortunate state.*

Empty
One whose life lacks meaning.

Expatriate
*One who lives outside his
native country.*

Tramp
*One who travels from place to
place on foot as a vagrant.*

Vile
One who is morally bad, or wicked.

Expelled
*One who is forced out and
deprived of membership.*

Fugitive
One who is in hiding to avoid arrest.

Alienated
One who feels estranged.

Out Castes may
endure **long**
periods of
quiescence,
obscurity, and
even **disgrace.**

—Timothy Leary
Intelligence Agents

4

He's a Madman!

*There is ominous tendency to call "insane" those
we don't agree with.*

—Timothy Leary

President Richard Nixon called Timothy Leary "the most
dangerous man alive" because he constantly encouraged
youth to question authority.

Leary taught that what we accept as objective reality is
only a construction of our minds. The only way to realize our
true selves is to question everything we have learned from
parents, teachers, politicians.
Socrates' approach, the Soc-
ratic Method— "knowledge
of not-knowing"—questions
unquestioned "truths" and to
keep questioning until students
discover for themselves that they
actually "know nothing" in the
sense of absolute knowledge.

Leary's approach provoked
people to question their models
of reality imposed by authorities,
encouraging them "to create their
own funnier, sexier, more opti-
mistic realities."

Timothy Leary

5

GOD

In the ancient days, when the first quiver of speech came to my lips, I ascended the holy mountain and spoke unto God, saying, "Master, I am thy slave. Thy hidden will is my law and I shall obey thee for ever more."

But God made no answer, and like a mighty tempest passed away. And after a thousand years I ascended the holy mountain and again spoke unto God, saying, "Creator, I am thy creation. Out of clay hast thou fashioned me and to thee I owe mine all."

And God made no answer, but like a thousand swift wings passed away. And after a thousand years I climbed the holy mountain and spoke unto God again, saying, "Father, I am thy son. In pity and love thou hast given me birth, and through love and worship I shall inherit thy kingdom."

And God made no answer, and like the mist that veils the distant hills he passed away. And after a thousand years I climbed the sacred mountain and again spoke unto God, saying, "My God, my aim and my fulfillment; I am thy yesterday and thou art my tomorrow. I am thy root in the earth and thou art my flower in the sky, and together we grow before the face of the sun."

Then God leaned over me, and in my ears whispered words of sweetness, and even as the sea that enfoldeth a brook that runneth down to her, he enfolded me.

And when I descended to the valleys and the plains, God was there also.

From The Prophet

Your daily life is your temple and your religion. Whenever you enter into it take with you your all.

And if you would know God be not therefore a solver of riddles.

Rather look about you and you shall see Him playing with your children.

And look into space; you shall see Him walking in the cloud, outstretching His arms in the lightning and descending in rain.

You shall see Him smiling in flowers, then rising and waving His hands in trees.

Gibran explores masklessness—madness—before God, where one can be neither slave, creature, nor child. One can only be equal to God, not in a frivolous egoistic sense but in terms of identify of being and substance, for to lose the contrived masks of society is to reveal the divine power in the universe and the self. Among others, therefore, we inevitably become estranged and incompatible.

To lose the masks of society is to reveal divine power.

Horror is the removal of masks.

—Robert Bloch

Psycho

6

God is Dead!

by Friedrich Nietzsche

Did you hear of the madman who lighted a lantern on a bright morning and ran to the market-place calling out unceasingly: "I seek God! I seek God!"

Many people standing about did not believe in God, so the madman caused a great deal of amusement. "Why! Is he lost?" one laughed. "Has he strayed away like a child?" asked another. "Or does he keep himself hidden? Is he afraid of us? Has he taken a sea-voyage? Has he emigrated?" And the people cried out laughingly, all in a hubbub.

The madman jumped into their midst, transfixing them with his piercing glances. "Where has God gone?" they cried out.

Nietzsche

"I tell you this: We have killed him—you and I!" the madman retorted. "We are murderers! But how did we do it? How were we able to drink up the sea? Who gave us the sponge to wipe away the whole horizon? What did we do when we loosened this earth from its sun? Whither does it now move? Whither do we move? Away from all suns? Do we not dash on unceasingly? Back-wards, sideways, forwards, in all directions? Is there still an above and below? Do we not stray, as through infinite nothingness? Does not empty space breathe upon us? Has it not become colder? Does not night come on continually, darker and darker? Shall we not have to light lanterns in the morning? Do we not hear the noise of the grave-diggers who are burying God? Do we not smell the divine decomposition—for even Gods decompose! God is dead! God remains dead! We killed him!"

"How shall we comfort ourselves, we murderers of all murders! How can we console ourselves—we the most murderous of all murderers? The holiest and the mightiest that the world has hitherto possessed, has bled to death under our knife. Who will wipe the blood off of us? What water is there for us to clean ourselves? What festivals of atonement, what sacred games shall we have to devise? Must we not ourselves become Gods, merely to seem worthy of it? There never was a greater deed. Whomever is born after us belong to a higher history than any history hitherto!"

The madman fell silent, as he looked at his listeners; they, too, were silent as they stared back at him in awe. Then he threw the lantern on the ground, so that it broke in pieces and was extinguished. "I came too early," he yelled back st them, "I have come too early. This prodigious event is in the future, yet to come—it has not yet reached your ears. Lightning and thunder need time, the light of the stars needs time, deeds need time—even after they are done—to be seen and understood. This deed is as yet further from you than the furthest star—*yet you have done it to yourselves!*"

That same day, the madman forced his way into churches and intoned his *Requiem æternam deo.* As he was captured and led out, he called out: "What are these churches now, if they are not the tombs and monuments of God?"

From Project Gutenberg public domain, "The Parable of the Madman", from The Joyful Wisdom" Friedrich Wilhelm Nietzsche, Third Book, No 125, pg. 168.

What Did Nietzache Mean?

What did Nietzsche mean when he said that God is dead?
Nietzsche had become an athiest and, having been raised in an
intensely devout and restrictivefamily atmosphere, we would
expect him to welcome "The Death of God!"

Nietzsche saw that humanity had indeed killed God—or the
notion of God. With the Renaissance, gifted individuals recov-
ered something of the ancient Greek way of thinking, which set
aside myth, superstition, and revelation and focused on what a
person could learn for themselves—God was not needed.

When Nietzsche declared the death of God, people didn't
understand the implication. Nietzsche actually believed that
recognition that God is Dead would lead to a moral crisis.
Nietzsche realized that spirituality is necessary to find meaning
in life. While Nietzsche, himself, had a problem with the institu-
tion of Christianity, he admired Jesus.

Nietzsche wasn't trying to get people to stop believing.
Rather he meant to emphasize the significance of losing faith.
Nietzsche was warning that if God is dead—really truly dead,
entirely discounted—then everything will change.What Nietzsche was saying *was* not that God is dead so let's throw a
party, rather he was saying that God is dead and he must be
replaced with something.

In the post-Enlightenment world, faith in God had been
replaced with faith in science. But Nietzsche, himself an atheist,
understood that we cannot live a faith-free life. God is dead, so
what must we do to find meaning for our lives without God?

"The holiest and the mightiest that the world has hitherto
possessed, has bled to death under our knife. Who will wipe
this blood off us? What water is there for us to clean ourselves?
What festivals of atonement, what sacred games shall we have to
invent? Is not the greatness of this deed too great for us? Must we
ourselves not become gods simply to appear worthy of it?"

Even though an athiest, Nietzsche knew that life must be meaningful and understood that life cannot be lived apart from a spiritual pursuit. We develop "festivals of atonement" or "sacred games" to replace old, dead religions. Even an atheist fills life with liturgy.

Nietzsche's spiritual alternative to God was formed from a fascination with the science of the world around us. We find meaning for our lives by jumping into the wonderous world around us. For Nietzsche, vitality itself was the meaning of life.

"I teach you, the overman [superman]. Man is something that shall be overcome. What have you done to overcome him?

Behold, I teach you the overman. The overman is the meaning of the earth. Let your will say: the overman shall be the meaning of the earth! I beseech you, my brothers, remain faithful to the earth, and do not believe those who speak to you of otherworldly hopes! Poison-mixers are they, whether they know it or not. Despisers of life are they, decaying and poisoned themselves, of whom the earth is weary: so let them go.

"Once the sin against God was the greatest sin; but God died, and these sinners died with him. To sin against the earth is now the most dreadful thing, and to esteem the entrails of the unknowable higher than the meaning of the earth.

—Nietzsche

About Nietzsche, Gilbran said:

"What a man! What a man! Alone he fought the whole world in the name of his Superman; and though the world forced him out of his reason in the end, yet did he whip it well. He died a Superman among pygmies, a sane madman in the midst of a world too decorously insane to be mad."

7

My Friend

My friend, I am not what I seem. Seeming is but a garment I wear—a care-woven garment that protects me from thy questionings and thee from my negligence. The "I" in me, my friend, dwells in the house of silence, and therein it shall remain for ever more, unperceived, unapproachable.

I would not have thee believe in what I say nor trust in what I do—for my words are naught but thy own thoughts in sound and my deeds thy own hopes in action.

When thou sayest, "The wind bloweth eastward," I say, "Aye, it doth blow east-ward"; for I would not have thee know that my mind doth not dwell upon the wind but upon the sea.

Thou canst not understand my seafaring thoughts, nor would I have thee understand. I would be at sea alone.

When it is day with thee, my friend, it is night with me; yet even then I speak of the noontide that dances upon the hills and of the purple shadow that steals its way across the valley; for thou canst not hear the songs of my darkness nor see my wings beating against the stars—and I fain would not have thee hear or see. I would be with night alone.

When thou ascendest to thy Heaven I descend to my Hell— even then thou callest to me across the unbridgeable gulf, "My companion, my comrade," and I call back to thee, "My comrade, my companion"—for I would not have thee see my Hell. The flame would burn thy eyesight and the smoke would crowd thy nostrils. And I love my Hell too well to have thee visit it. I would be in Hell alone. Thou lovest Truth and Beauty and

Righteousness; and I for thy sake say it is well and seemly to love these things. But in my heart I laugh at thy love. Yet I would not have thee see my laughter. I would laugh alone.

My friend, thou art good and cautious and wise; nay, thou art perfect—and I, too, speak with thee wisely and cautiously. And yet I am mad. But I mask my madness. I would be mad alone.

My friend, thou art not my friend, but how shall I make thee understand? My path is not thy path, yet together we walk, hand in hand.

Nowhere does Gibran's genius shine more luminously than in his exploration of identity and the masks behind which we hide our innermost selves from others and even from ourselves; the authentic, vulnerable self that he so beautifully describes as

"a human chaos, a nebula of confused elements," "a green seed of unfulfilled passion, a mad tempest that seeketh neither east nor west, a bewildered fragment from a burnt planet."

Gibran explores the interplay between being vs. appearing and our impulse for self-display, between our seeming selves and our being selves.

I am not who I seem to be.

The "friend" Gibran addresses is the idealized self, the self we present to the world, the aspirational self of who we would like to be rather than who we are—a self that invariably obscures our incompleteness and imperfection, which are the wellspring of our richest humanity.

Gibran writes:

My friend, thou art good and cautious and wise; nay, thou art perfect—and I, too, speak with thee wisely and cautiously. And yet I am mad. But I mask my madness. I would be mad alone. My friend, thou art not my friend, but how shall I make thee understand? My path is not thy path, yet together we walk, hand in hand.

This is how the Madman—the hermit must live, not in antagonism or controversy but alone and separate, in silence. Not donning a new mask, the poet instead demurs and disengages and lets the other go their way, safeguarding his own path.

8

I'm a Phony and a Fraud!

Coined in 1978 by psychologists Clance and Imes, "The Impostor Syndrome" describes people marked by an inability to internalize their accomplishments and an intense fear of being exposed as a fraud or phony. Affecting men and women equally, people suffering the syndrome are convinced that they are frauds and do not deserve the success they have achieved. They dismiss proof of success as luck, timing, or deception.

Gifted people are generally hard-working, which tends to bring more praise and success, perpetuating fears of being "found out". The victims tend to believe they must work extra hard, so they over-prepare, tinker and obsess over details. Gifted people often use charm to gain approval and praise

The Imposter Syndrome describes people with an intense fear of being exposed as a fraud or phony.

from supervisors. Yet, when the supervisor gives recognition, they feel that it is based on charm and not on ability.

The impostor syndrome is not a mental disorder, rather it is an acquired, i.e., learned, personality trait. Signs that someone may be feeling like an impostor include perfectionism, work-alcoholism, sabotaging achievements, intense fear of failing, and discounting praise. It is accompanied by anxiety, stress, and/or depression.

Victims tend to give the answers they believe superiors want, which exacerbates the feelings of "being a fake". When shown evidence of their competence, they tend to doubt themselves even more.

In other cases, victim may believe they must discount themselves to be accepted. Research results estimate that about 40 percent of successful people consider themselves to be frauds, and that more than 70 percent of all people feel like an imposter at some time.

A study by Queena Hoang suggested that people of color may experience the impostor syndrome as a result of suspecting they were given their position by affirmative action and not based upon their ability. A study conducted at the University of Texas in 2013 showed that Asian-American college students are more likely than African-American or Latino students to expe-

rience feelings of being an impostor. Identifying these students can be difficult because those who express feeling symptoms of impostor syndrome are "often the most energetic, bright, and hardworking students amongst their peers".

To be accepted, I wear a mask.

The most effective intervention is to discuss imposter feelings with peers. People who experience impostor syndrome are generally unaware that others also feel inadequate. When addressed, victims no longer feel alone in their negative experience.

Making a list of accomplishments, positive feedback and success stories can help. Finally, developing a strong support system that provides feedback on performance and has discussions about impostor syndrome on a regular basis is very helpful.

Keeping a personal journal can be very beneficial because it allows the victim to organize thoughts in writing. The written record of objective accomplishments can enable the person to associate those accomplishments with reality, rather than simply dismissing them.

9

On the Meaning of Alienation

Sociologist Melvin Seeman provided a robust definition of social alienation in a paper published in 1959, titled "On the Meaning of Alienation." The five features Seeman attributed to social alienation hold true today.

Features of social alienation:

1. **Powerlessness**: People believe what happens in their lives is outside of their control, and that what they do does not matter. They believe they do not have the power to shape their life course.

2. **Meaninglessness**: People do not derive meaning from the things in which they engage.

3. **Normlessness** – Expectations for one's behavior has eroded and there is little sense of what is right and wrong.

4. **Social isolation**: People do not feel meaningfully connected to their community through shared values, beliefs, and practices.

5. **Self-estrangement**: People experiencing social alienation deny their own personal interests and desires in order to satisfy demands placed by others and social norms.

Karl Marx

Causes of Social Alienation

Alienation was central to Karl Marx's critique of industrial capitalism and the class stratified social system, which refers to the way people are ranked and ordered in society. According to Marx, the organization of the capitalist system of production features a wealthy class of owners and managers who purchase labor from workers for wages, creating the alienation of the entire working class. The economic instability and the social upheaval that tends to go with capitalism leads to anomie—a sense of normlessness that fosters social alienation.

Social alienation is a breakdown of the ties that bind people together to make a functional society—a state of social derangement. Periods of anomie are unstable, chaotic, and often rife with conflict because the social force of the norms and values that otherwise provide stability is weakened or missing.

Social alienation can result from the experience of living at the lower rungs of social hierarchies of race and class. Many people of color experience social alienation as a consequence of systemic racism. People who live in poverty experience social isolation because they are economically unable to participate in society in a way that is considered normal. Social alienation is a condition in social relationships reflected by a low degree of integration or common values and a high degree of distance or isolation between individuals, or between an individual and a group of people in a community or work environment.

The production of too many useful things results in too many useless people.

—Karl Marx

10

Ostracism

Ostracism (Greek: ὀστρακισμός, ostrakismos) was a proce-
dure under the Athenian democracy in which any citizen
could be expelled from the city-state of Athens for ten years.

While some instances clearly expressed popular anger at the
citizen, ostracism was often used preemptively as a way of neutralizing someone thought to be a threat to the state or potential
tyrant. It has been called an "honourable exile" by scholar P. J.
Rhodes.

The word "ostracism" continues to be used for various cases
of social shunning.

*Ostracism was used as a way of neutralizing someone
thought to be a threat to the state.*

11

The Scarecrow

Once I said to a scarecrow, "You must be tired of standing in this lonely field."

And he said, "The joy of scaring is a deep and lasting one, and I never tire of it."

Said I, after a minute of thought, "It is true; for I too have known that joy."

Said he, "Only those who are stuffed with straw can know it."

Then I left him, not knowing whether he had complimented or belittled me.

A year passed, during which the scarecrow turned philosopher.

And when I passed by him again I saw two crows building a nest under his hat.

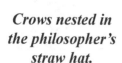

Crows nested in the philosopher's straw hat.

12

The Sleep-Walkers

In the town where I was born lived a woman and her daughter, who walked in their sleep.

One night, while silence enfolded the world, the woman and her daughter, walking, yet asleep, met in their mist-veiled garden.

And the mother spoke, and she said: "At last, at last, my enemy! You by whom my youth was destroyed—who have built up your life upon the ruins of mine! Would I could kill you!"

And the daughter spoke, and she said: "O hateful woman, selfish and old! Who stand between my freer self and me! Who would have my life an echo of your own faded life! Would you were dead!"

At that moment a cock crew, and both women awoke. The mother said gently, "Is that you, darling?" And the daughter answered gently, "Yes, dear."

A mother and daughter speak their hatred of one another in their somnolence, but upon awakening put on their masks to greet one another in sweet tones.

13

The Wise Dog

One day there passed by a company of cats a wise dog.

And as he came near and saw that they were very intent and heeded him not, he stopped.

Then there arose in the midst of the company a large, grave cat and looked upon them and said, "Brethren, pray ye; and when ye have prayed again and yet again, nothing doubting, verily then it shall rain mice."

And when the dog heard this he laughed in his heart and turned from them saying, "O blind and foolish cats, has it not been written and have I not known and my fathers before me, that that which raineth for prayer and faith and supplication is not mice but bones."

Foolish cats! Prayer rains bones, not mice.

14

The Two Hermits

Upon a lonely mountain, there lived two hermits who worshipped God and loved one another.

Now these two hermits had one earthen bowl, and this was their only possession.

One day an evil spirit entered into the heart of the older hermit and he came to the younger and said, "It is long that we have lived together. The time has come for us to part. Let us divide our possessions."

Divide it!.

Then the younger hermit was saddened and he said, "It grieves me, Brother, that thou shouldst leave me. But if thou must needs go, so be it," and he brought the earthen bowl and gave it to him saying, "We cannot divide it, Brother, let it be thine."

Then the older hermit said, "Charity I will not accept. I will take nothing but mine own. It must be divided."

And the younger one said, "If the bowl be broken, of what use would it be to thee or to me? If it be thy pleasure let us rather cast a lot."

But the older hermit said again, "I will have but justice and mine own, and I will not trust justice and mine own to vain chance. The bowl must be divided." Then the younger hermit could reason no further and he said, "If it be indeed thy will, and if even so thou wouldst have it let us now break the bowl." But the face of the older hermit grew exceeding dark, and he cried, "O thou cursed coward, thou wouldst not fight."

15

On Giving and Taking

Once there lived a man who had a valleyful of needles.

And one day the mother of Jesus came to him and said: "Friend, my son's garment is torn and I must needs mend it before he goeth to the temple. Wouldst thou not give me a needle?"

And he gave but he gave her not a needle, her a learned discourse on Giving and Taking to carry to her son before he should go to the temple.

He gave her a discourse on giving and taking, but no needle.

16

Be Nice!

Five hundred years ago, when nice was first used in English, it meant "foolish or stupid." This is not as surprising as it may seem, since it came through early French from the Latin *nescius*, meaning "ignorant."

From there it embraced many a negative quality, including wantonness, extravagance, and ostentation, as well as cowardice and sloth. In the Middle Ages it took on the more neutral attributes of shyness and reserve. By the 16th Century, the sense of being "very particular" or "finicky" had developed.

It was society's admiration of such qualities in the 18th Century that brought on the more positively charged meanings of 'nice' that had been vying for a place for much of the word's history, and the values of respectability and virtue began to take over. Such positive associations remain today, when the main meaning of 'nice' is 'pleasant'.

Nice Guy

A term in popular culture describing a pleasant, likable male who goes out of his way to avoid confrontations, to do favors, give emotional support, with friendly yet unassertive personal traits.

Associate yourself with people of good quality, for it is better to be alone than in bad company.

17

The Seven Selves

In the silent hour of the night, as I lay half asleep, my seven selves sat together and thus conversed in whispers:

First Self: Here, in this madman, I have dwelt all these years, with naught to do but renew his pain by day and recreate his sorrow by night. I can bear my fate no longer, and now I must rebel.

Gibran's seven selves.

Second Self: Yours is a better lot than mine, brother, for it is given me to be this madman's joyous self. I laugh his laughter and sing his happy hours, and with thrice winged feet I dance his brighter thoughts. It is I that would rebel against my weary existence.

Third Self: And what of me, the love-ridden self, the flaming brand of wild passion and fantastic desires? It is I the love-sick self who would rebel against this madman.

Fourth Self: I, amongst you all, am the most miserable, for naught was given me but the odious hatred and destructive

loathing. It is I, the tempest-like self, the one born in the black caves of Hell, who would protest against serving this madman.

> *God said, "Love your enemy".*
> *I obeyed and loved myself.*
>
> —Khalil Gibran

Fifth Self: Nay, it is I, the thinking self, the fanciful self, the self of hunger and thirst, the one doomed to wander without rest in search of unknown things and things not yet created; it is I, not you, who would rebel.

Sixth Self: And I, the working self, the pitiful labourer, who, with patient hands, and longing eyes, fashion the days into images and give the formless elements new and eternal forms—it is I, the solitary one, who would rebel against this restless madman.

Seventh Self: How strange that you all would rebel against this man, because each and every one of you has a preordained fate to fulfill. Ah! could I but be like one of you, a self with a determined lot! But I have none, I am the do-nothing self, the one who sits in the dumb, empty no-where and nowhen, when you are busy recreating life. Is it you or I, neighbors, who should rebel?

When the seventh self thus spoke the other six selves looked with pity upon him but said nothing more; and as the night grew deeper one after the other went to sleep enfolded with a new and happy submission. But the seventh self remained watching and gazing at nothingness, which is behind all things.

The selves complain about their assigned functions: the joyous self, the love-ridden self, the passion-filled tempestuous self, the fanciful self. The do-nothing self, complains that the others are busy while he sits in "empty nowhere and nowhen." The other selves have a purpose, while he is quietly reconciled,and stays up after the others sleep, "watching and gazing at nothingness, which is behind all things."

18

The Mad Woman

by Guy de Maupassant

Monsieur d'Endolin said, "I can tell you a terrible story about the Franco-Prussian war," to some friends assembled in the smoking-room of Baron de Ravot's chateau. "You know my house in the Faubourg de Cormeil, I was living there when the Prussians came, and I had for a neighbor a kind of mad woman, who had lost her senses in consequence of a series of misfortunes. At the age of seven and twenty she had lost her father, her husband, and her newly born child, all in the space of a month.

"When death has once entered into a house, it almost invariably

She merely turned her vague eyes on him, without replying.

returns immediately, as if it knew the way, and the young woman, overwhelmed with grief, took to her bed and was delirious for six weeks. Then a species of calm lassitude succeeded that violent crisis, and she remained motionless, eating next to nothing, and only moving her eyes. Every time they tried to make her get up, she screamed as if they were about to kill her, and so they ended by leaving her continually in bed, and only taking her out to wash her, to change her linen, and to turn her mattress.

"An old servant remained with her, to give her something to drink, or a little cold meat, from time to time. What passed in that despairing mind? No one ever knew, for she did not speak at all now. Was she thinking of the dead? Was she dreaming sadly, without any precise recollection of anything that had happened? Or was her memory as stagnant as water without any current? But however this may have been, for fifteen years she remained thus inert and secluded.

"The war broke out, and in the beginning of December the Germans came to Cormeil. I can remember it as if it were but yesterday. It was freezing hard enough to split the stones, and I myself was lying back in an armchair, being unable to move on account of the gout, when I heard their heavy and regular tread, and could see them pass from my window.

"They defiled past interminably, with that peculiar motion of a puppet on wires, which belongs to them. Then the officers billeted their men on the inhabitants, and I had seventeen of them. My neighbor, the crazy woman, had a dozen, one of whom was the Commandant, a regular violent, surly swashbuckler.

"During the first few days, everything went on as usual. The officers next door had been told that the lady was ill, and they did not trouble themselves about that in the least, but soon that woman whom they never saw irritated them. They asked what her illness was, and were told that she had been in bed for fifteen years, in consequence of terrible grief. No doubt they did not believe it, and thought that the poor mad creature would not leave her bed out of pride, so that she might not come near the Prussians, or speak to them or even see them.

"The Commandant insisted upon her receiving him. He was shown into the room and said to her roughly: 'I must beg you to get up, Madame, and to come downstairs so that we may all see you.' But she merely turned her vague eyes on him, without replying, and so he continued: 'I do not intend to tolerate any insolence, and if you do not get up of your own accord, I can easily find means to make you walk without any assistance.'

"But she did not give any signs of having heard him, and remained quite motionless. Then he got furious, taking that calm silence for a mark of supreme contempt; so he added: 'If you do not come downstairs tomorrow—' And then he left the room.

"The next day the terrified old servant wished to dress her, but the mad woman began to scream violently, and resisted with all her might. The officer ran upstairs quickly, and the servant threw herself at his feet and cried: 'She will not come down, Monsieur, she will not. Forgive her, for she is so unhappy.'

"The soldier was embarrassed, as in spite of his anger, he did not venture to order his soldiers to drag her out. But suddenly he began to laugh, and gave some orders in German, and soon a party of soldiers was seen coming out supporting a mattress as if they were carrying a wounded man. On that bed, which had not been unmade, the mad woman, who was still silent, was lying quite quietly, for she was quite indifferent to anything that went on, as long as they let her lie. Behind her, a soldier was carrying a parcel of feminine attire, and the officer said, rubbing his hands: 'We will just see whether you cannot dress yourself alone, and take a little walk.'

"And then the procession went off in the direction of the forest of Imauville; in two hours the soldiers came back alone, and nothing more was seen of the mad woman. What had they done with her? Where had they taken her to? No one knew.

"The snow was falling day and night, and enveloped the plain and the woods in a shroud of frozen foam, and the wolves came and howled at our very doors.

"The thought of that poor lost woman haunted me, and I made several applications to the Prussian authorities in order to obtain some information, and was nearly shot for doing so. When spring returned, the army of occupation withdrew, but my neighbor's house remained closed, and the grass grew thick in the garden walks. The old servant had died during the winter, and nobody troubled any longer about the occurrence; I alone thought about it constantly. What had they done with the woman? Had she escaped through the forest? Had somebody found her, and taken her to a hospital, without being able to obtain any information from her? Nothing happened to relieve my doubts; but by degrees, time assuaged my fears.

"Well, in the following autumn the woodcock were very plentiful, and as my gout had left me for a time, I dragged myself as far as the forest. I had already killed four or five of the long-billed birds, when I knocked over one which fell into a ditch full of branches, and I was obliged to get into it, in order to pick it up, and I found that it had fallen close to a dead, human body. Immediately the recollection of the mad woman struck me like a blow in the chest. Many other people had perhaps died in the woods during that disastrous year, but though I do not know why, I was sure, sure, I tell you, that I should see the head of that wretched maniac.

"And suddenly I understood, I guessed everything. They had abandoned her on that mattress in the cold, deserted wood; and, faithful to her fixed idea, she had allowed herself to perish under that thick and light counterpane of snow, without moving either arms or legs.

"Then the wolves had devoured her, and the birds had built their nests with the wool from her torn bed, and I took charge of her bones. I only pray that our sons may never see any wars again."

They left her in the snow for the wolves.

From: The Entire Original Maupassant Short Stories, by Guy de Maupassant. Project Gutenberg, Public Domain.

19

War

One night a feast was held in the palace, and there came a man who prostrated himself before the prince, and all the feasters looked upon him; and they saw that one of his eyes was out and that the empty socket bled.

And the prince inquired of him, "What has befallen you?" And the man replied, "O Prince, I am by profession a thief, and last night, because there was no moon, I went to rob the moneychanger's shop, and as I climbed in through the window I made a mistake and entered the weaver's shop, and in the dark I ran into the weaver's loom and my eye was plucked out. And now, O Prince, I ask for justice upon the weaver." Then the prince sent for the weaver and he came, and it was decreed that one of his eyes should be plucked out.

"O Prince," said the weaver, "the decree is just. It is right that one of my eyes be taken. And yet, alas! both are necessary to me in order that I may see the two sides of the cloth that I weave. But I have a neighbor, a cobbler, who has also two eyes, and in his trade both eyes are not necessary."

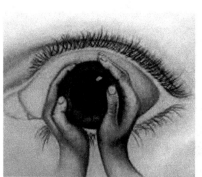

They took out the cobbler's eye and justice was done.

Then the prince sent for the cobbler. And he came. And they took out one of the cobbler's two eyes. And justice was satisfied.

20

The Fox

A fox looked at his shadow at sunrise and said, "I will have a camel for lunch today."

And all morning he went about looking for camels. But at noon he saw his shadow again—and he said, "A mouse will do."

At sunrise his shadow was a camel but by noon it became a mouse.

21

The Wise King

Once there ruled in the distant city of Wirani a king who was both mighty and wise. And he was feared for his might and loved for his wisdom.

Now, in the heart of that city was a well, whose water was cool and crystalline, from which all the inhabitants drank, even the king and his courtiers; for there was no other well.

One night when all were asleep, a witch entered the city, and poured seven drops of strange liquid into the well, and said, "From this hour he who drinks this water shall become mad."

Next morning all the inhabitants, save the king and his lord chamberlain, drank from the well and became mad, even as the witch had foretold.

The king was feared for his might and loved for his wisdom.

And during that day the people in the narrow streets and in the market places did naught but whisper to one another, "The king is mad. Our king and his lord chamberlain have lost their reason. Surely we cannot be ruled by a mad king. We must dethrone him."

That evening the king ordered a golden goblet to be filled from the well. And when it was brought to him he drank deeply, and gave it to his lord chamberlain to drink.

And there was great rejoicing in that distant city of Wirani, because its king and its lord chamberlain had regained their reason.

The press for conformity absorbs society like nothing else. Here a witch poisons the city well with a draught that causes madness, and those who do not drink remain sane. The people rebel against the king and his chamberlain, who have not drunk the water, calling them mad. But when the latter do drink, the people rejoice because now their ruler and chamberlain have regained their reason.

They rejoiced when the king drank and was no longer mad.

22

Ridicule

"Ridicule is man's most potent weapon."

– Saul Alinsky
Rules for Radicals

R idicule is the use of unkind words to make someone or something look stupid. Ridicule subjects someone or something to contemptuous and dismissive language to deride and mock. Ridicule taunts and makes fun of a person, in an unkind, jeering way with the intention of humiliating, by using sarcasm, satire, and irony.

To crush your opponent's spirit, find ways to mock, denigrate, and ridicule that person—especially with moral arguments.

The dispair is there; now it's up to us to go in and rub raw the sores of discontent, to galvanize them for radical social change.

—Saul Alinsky

23

Disdain, Scorn, Belittle

Disdain is communicating that one is unworthy of consideration. Synonyms include scorn, derision, pour scorn on, regard with contempt, sneer at, sniff at, curl one's lip at, look down one's nose at, and belittle.

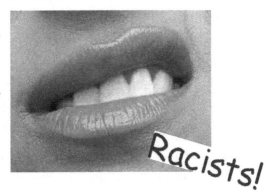

The lip corner is tightened and raised on one side of the face.

To belittle, you have to be little.

—Khalil Gibran

24

Ambition

Three men met at a tavern table. One was a weaver, another a carpenter and the third a ploughman.

Said the weaver, "I sold a fine linen shroud today for two pieces of gold. Let us have all the wine we want."

"And I," said the carpenter, "I sold my best coffin. We will have a great roast with the wine."

"I only dug a grave," said the ploughman, "but my patron paid me double. Let us have honey cakes, too."

And all that evening the tavern was busy, for they called often for wine and meat and cakes. And they were merry.

And the host rubbed his hands and smiled at his wife; for his guests were spending freely.

When they left the moon was high, and they walked along the road singing and shouting together.

The three men celebrated their good fortune.

The host and his wife stood in the tavern door and looked after them. "Ah!" said the wife, "these gentlemen! So freehanded and so gay! If only they could bring us such luck every day! Then our son need not be a tavern-keeper and work hard. We could educate him, and he could become a priest."

The tavern-keeper's wife relishes a death that brings largesse from those who profit—the shroud-weaver, the coffin-maker, the grave-digger.

The Tavern-Keeper.

25

The New Pleasure

Last night I invented a new pleasure, and as I was giving it the first trial when an angel and a devil came rushing toward my house. They met at my door and fought with each other over my newly created pleasure; the one crying, "It is a sin!" —the other, "It is a virtue!"

They fought over my pleasure.

Khalil Gibran

26

The Other Language

Three days after I was born, as I lay in my silken cradle, gazing with astonished dismay on the new world round about me, my mother spoke to the wet-nurse, saying, "How is my child?"

And the wet-nurse answered, "He does well madam, I have fed him three times; and never before have I seen a babe so young yet so gay."

And I was indignant; and I cried, "It is not true, mother; for my bed is hard, and the milk I have sucked is bitter to my mouth, and the odor of the breast is foul in my nostrils, and I am most miserable."

But my mother did not understand, nor did the nurse; for the language I spoke was that of the world from which I came.

The Language Tree.

And on the twenty-first day of my life, as I was being christened, the priest said to my mother, "You should indeed be happy, madam, that your son was born a Christian."

And I was surprised, and I said to the priest, "Then your mother in Heaven should be unhappy, for you were not born a Christian." But the priest too did not understand my language.

And after seven moons, one day a soothsayer looked at me, and he said to my mother, "Your son will be a statesman and a great leader of men." But I cried out, "That is a false prophecy; for I shall be a musician, and naught but a musician shall I be."

But even at that age my language was not understood—and great was my astonshment.

And after three and thirty years, during which my mother, and the nurse, and the priest have all died, (the shadow of God be upon their spirits) the soothsayer still lives. And yesterday I met him near the gate of the temple; and while we were talking together he said, "I have always known you would become a great musician. Even in your infancy I prophesied and foretold your future." And I believed him—for now I too have forgotten the language of that other world.

27

Control the Past

"Who controls the past controls the future. Who controls the present controls the past."

—George Orwell

Nineteen Eighty-Four [1984]

This Party slogan appears twice in *1984,* George Orwell's disturbing novel of a dark and threatening future. "Who controls the past controls the future" is one of Big Brother's—the ruling government—slogans. It is an example of the Party's technique of using fake history to break down the psychological independence of its subjects. Control of the past ensures control of the future, because the past can be treated essentially as a set of conditions that justify or encourage future goals: if the past was idyllic, then people will act to re-create it; if the past was nightmarish, then people will act to prevent such circumstances from recurring. The Party created a past that was a time of misery and slavery from which it claimed to have liberated the human race, thus compelling people to work toward the Party's goals.

The Party had complete political power so that it controlled the way in which its subjects think about and interpret the past: every history book reflected Party ideology, and individuals were forbidden from keeping mementos, such as photographs and documents. Consequently, Oceania citizens had a very short, fuzzy memory, and were willing to believe whatever the Party told them.

In the second appearance of this quote, O'Brien tells Winston that the past is real only in the minds of human beings and has no concrete existence. To which O'Brien argued that the

Party's version of the past was what people believe, so that past, while it has no basis in real events, is the truth.

Orwell's quote has an additional sinister ring to it, suggesting that whoever writes the history books affects the way we view the world and the way we will function in the future. Often it is government and government-supported businesses that publishes textbooks so they determine what is in them. It is from textbooks that the people learn about the past.

George Orwell, an English socialist whose real name was Eric Blair, was outraged by the suffering he witnessed in the Great Depression and in Stalin's Russia. While other prominent left-wing thinkers, such as HG Wells, accepted Stalin's regime at face value, Orwell denounced it as an appalling abuse.

Orwell had first hand experience of propaganda because he worked for the BBC throughout World War II and saw it's power to shape reality. He was disturbed to observe how Stalin's propaganda became an instrument of control, by editing factual records— much like the media today.

George Orwell

Winston Smith, the protagonist in *1984*, works at the Ministry of Truth, which exists to propagate the party line. An educated man, Smith spent his life falsifying evidence, and having done so, he destroyed the proof. He spent his days rewriting articles that might prove Big Brother was wrong or associated with people who have been purged and executed.

Written in the 1940s, Orwell's novel was directed at totalitarian regimes, but his thesis stands, today even in social media. The ability to create fake news—control the debate, to limit access to information can create a dangerous narrative. Tyranny begins and ends with control of the imagination. Memory is our best defense.

28

The Pomegranate

Once when I was living in the heart of a pomegranate, I heard a seed saying, "Someday I shall become a tree, and the wind will sing in my branches, and the sun will dance on my leaves, and I shall be strong and beautiful through all the seasons."

Then another seed spoke and said, "When I was as young as you, I too held such views; but now that I can weigh and measure things, I see that my hopes were vain."

And a third seed spoke also, "I see in us nothing that promises so great a future."

And a fourth said, "But what a mockery our life would be, without a greater future!"

Said a fifth, "Why dispute what we shall be, when we know not even what we are."

I was living in the heart of a pomegranate where the seeds were noisy, so I moved into quince where the seeds were few and almost silent.

But a sixth replied, "Whatever we are, that we shall continue to be." And a seventh said, "I have such a clear idea how everything will be, but I cannot put it into words."

Then an eighth spoke—and a ninth—and a tenth— and then many—until all were speaking, and I could distinguish nothing for the many voices. And so I moved that very day into the heart of a quince, where the seeds are few and almost silent.

A similar device as used in the Seven Selves of multiple complainers appears in "The Pomegranate," again representing the multiple thoughts and chatter of society as well as the mind. Gibran shows that achieving an equilibrium and silence in the mind is a necessary prelude to wisdom.

The narrator lives within this fruit but the many seeds begin jabbering their views of life and the universe until a cacophony is raised and the narrator happily goes to live in a quince, "where the seeds are few, and almost silent." The cacophony may be in our own heads from listening to others or from listening to ourselves. The society of others is as bad as the society of an undisciplined mind. There is no alternative but to seek silence.

The seeds spoke.

29

The Two Cages

In my father's garden there are two cages. In one is a lion, which my father's slaves brought from the desert of Ninavah; in the other is a song-less sparrow. Every day at dawn the sparrow calls to the lion, "Good morrow to thee, brother prisoner."

Each dawn the sparrow calls to the lion in the next cage.

30

The Three Ants

Three ants met on the nose of a man who was lying asleep in the sun. And after they had saluted one another, each according to the custom of his tribe, they stood there conversing.

The first ant said, "These hills and plains are the most barren I have known. I have searched all day for a grain of some sort, and there is none to be found."

Said the second ant, "I too have found nothing, though I have visited every nook and glade. This is, I believe, what my people call the soft, moving land where nothing grows."

Then the third ant raised his head and said, "My friends, we are standing now on the nose of the Supreme Ant, the mighty and infinite Ant, whose body is so great that we cannot see it, whose shadow is so vast that we cannot trace it, whose voice is so loud that we cannot hear it; and He is omnipresent." When the third ant spoke

Three ants stood on the nose of the Supreme Ant.

thus the other ants looked at each other and laughed. At that moment the man moved and in his sleep raised his hand and scratched his nose, and the three ants were crushed.

31

The Grave-Digger

Once, as I was burying one of my dead selves, the grave-digger came by and said to me, "Of all those who come here to bury, you alone I like." Said I, "You please me exceedingly, but why do you like me?" "Because," said he, "They come weeping and go weeping—you only come laughing and go laughing."

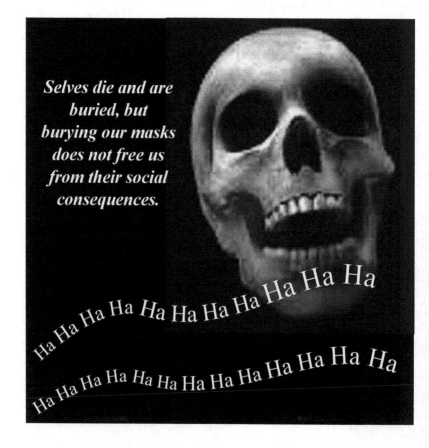

Selves die and are buried, but burying our masks does not free us from their social consequences.

Ha Ha Ha Ha Ha Ha Ha Ha Ha Ha Ha Ha

Ha Ha Ha Ha Ha Ha Ha Ha Ha Ha Ha Ha Ha Ha

32

On the Steps of the Temple

Yestereve, on the marble steps of the Temple, I saw a woman sitting between two men. One side of her face was pale, the other was blushing.

I saw a woman sitting on the Temple steps.

33

The Blessed City

In my youth I was told that in a certain city everyone lived according to the Scriptures.

And I said, "I will seek that city and the blessedness thereof." And it was far.

And I made great provision for my journey. And after forty days I beheld the city and on the forty-first day I entered into it.

And lo! The whole company of the inhabitants had each but a single eye and but one hand. And I was astonished and said to myself, "Shall they of this so holy city have but one eye and one hand?"

Then I saw that they too were astonished, for they were marveling greatly at my two hands and my two eyes.

And as they were speaking together I inquired of them saying, "Is this indeed the Blessed City, where each man lives according to the Scriptures?" And they said, "Yes, this is that city."

"And what," said I, "hath befallen you, and where are your right eyes and your right hands?"

There was a heap of hands and eyes—all withered.

"And what," said I, "hath befallen you, and where are your right eyes and your right hands?"

And all the people were moved. And they said, "Come thou and see."

A heap of eye-balls.

And they took me to the temple in the midst of the city. And in the temple I saw a heap of hands and eyes. All withered. Then said I, "Alas! What conqueror hath committed this cruelty upon you?"

And there went a murmur amongst them. And one of their elders stood forth and said, "This doing is of ourselves. God hath made us conquerors over the evil that was in us."

And he led me to a high altar, and all the people followed. And he showed me above the altar and inscription graven, and I read:

"If thy right eye offend thee, pluck it out and cast it from thee; for it is profitable for thee that one of thy members should perish, and not that thy whole body should be cast into hell. And if thy right hand offend thee, cut if off and cast it from thee; for it is profitable for thee that one of the members should perish, and not that thy whole body should be cast into hell."

Then I understood. And I turned about to all the people and cried, "Hath no man or woman among you two eyes or two hands?"

And they answered me saying, "No, not one. There is none whole save such as are yet too young to read the Scripture and to understand its commandment."

And when we had come out of the temple, I straightway left that Blessed City; for I was not too young, and I could read the scripture.

34

Pressure to Conform

Conformity is the tendency to align attitudes, beliefs, and behaviors with others. It's a powerful force that takes the form of overt social pressure as well as subtle unconscious influences. We humans like to think of ourselves as independently thinking but we are powerfully driven to fit in, which usually means going slong to get along.

Conformity is a process of matching attitudes, beliefs, and behaviors to the group. Norms are implicit, specific rules, shared by a group of individuals that guide their interactions. The tendency to conform occurs in small groups as well as in society as a whole, resulting from subtle unconscious influences and social pressure. Conformity can occur in the presence of others, or when an individual is alone.

People unwilling to conform risk being socially rejected. People tend to conform seeking security within a group, often referred to as groupthink—a pattern of conformity in thought and action to group values and ethics, ignoring realistic appraisal of other courses of action.

Conformity can be regarded as either good or bad. Conforming to driving laws would be considered beneficial conformity. By conforming in early childhood years we learn to adopt the appropriate behavior needed to interact and develop correctly in society. Conformity to social norms enables societies to function smoothly and predictably and is positive force that prevents disruptive or dangerous acts. Because conformity is a group phenomenon, factors such as group size, unanimity, cohesion, status, prior commitment and public opinion help determine the level of conformity an individual displays.

Conformity can manifest apathy towards others. Conforming means not questioning authority and putting blind trust in the leaders of society. Such blind trust can be dangerous when it comes to problems within society because conformity can breed a sense of "not my problem". Giving over one's power to the leaders can mean ignoring social justice issues because after all "they are the ones in charge and they should do something about it". Conformity can release the individual from feelings of outrage and the need for action over injustice.

Conformity breeds nonthinkers. Conformity can cause an unjust world. For example, when asked why they killed Jews, Nazi soldiers said "we were just following orders, revealing the danger of failing to question authority.

Conformity is necessary to ensure that society is successful, while nonconformity ensures that the leaders do not have too much power over the people. There are needs for rules and rule breakers for a system that is fluid and that can be changed when needed. Conformity is a good thing but we also need those who refuse to conform to every rule.

CONFORM
Everybody's doing it.

The balance between conforming and non-conforming is a tight rope. If there are too many nonconforming people society does not work, too many conformists risk that the power will be concentrated by a few. Power corrupts.

35

The Good God & the Evil God

The Good God and the Evil God met on the mountain top. The Good God said, "Good day to you, brother." The Evil God made no answer. And the Good God said, "You are in a bad humour today."

"Yes," said the Evil God, "for of late I have been often mistaken for you, called by your name, and treated as if I were you, and it ill-pleases me."

And the Good God said. "But I too have been mistaken for you and called by your name."

The Evil God walked away cursing the stupidity of man.

The Good God and the Evil God met.

36

Defeat

Defeat, my Defeat, my solitude and my aloofness; You are dearer to me than a thousand triumphs, and sweeter to my heart than all worldglory.

Defeat, my Defeat, my self-knowledge and my defiance, through you I know that I am yet young and swift of foot. and not to be trapped by withering laurels. And in you I have found aloneness and the joy of being shunned and scorned.

Defeat, my Defeat, my shining sword and shield. In your eyes I have read that to be enthroned is to be enslaved, and to be understood is to be levelled down, and to be grasped is but to reach one's fullness. snd like a ripe fruit to fall and be consumed.

Defeat, my Defeat, my bold companion, You shall hear my songs and my cries and my silences, and none but you shall speak to me of the beating of wings,

NEVER CONFUSE a single failure with a FINAL DEFEAT

and urging of seas, and of mountains that burn in the night, and you alone shall climb my steep and rocky soul.

Defeat, my Defeat, my deathless courage, you and I shall laugh together with the storm, and together we shall dig graves for all that die in us, and we shall stand in the sun with a will, and we shall be dangerous.

Gibran expresses a Nietzschean triumph of self-discovery in the sorrow and pain encountered on the path, that these defeats should instruct one on the nature of the world. Defeat informs the soul better than any teacher or instruction. Defeat brings the individual to confront the fullness of life and transmutes it for the self, making for a self that is stronger, more defiant, "dangerous."

37

Night & the Madman

"I am like thee, O, Night, dark and naked; I walk on the flaming path which is above my day-dreams, and whenever my foot touches earth a giant oaktree comes forth."

"Nay, thou art not like me, O, Madman, for thou still lookest backward to see how large a foot-print thou leavest on the sand."

"I am like thee, O, Night, silent and deep; and in the heart of my loneliness lies a Goddess in child-bed; and in him who is being born Heaven touches Hell."

"Nay, thou art not like me, O, Madman, for thou shudderest yet before pain, and the song of the abyss terrifies thee."

I am like thee, Night—dark and naked.

"I am like thee, O, Night, wild and terrible; for my ears are crowded with cries of conquered nations and sighs for forgotten lands."

"Nay, thou art not like me, O, Madman, for thou still takest thy little-self for a comrade, and with thy monster-self thou canst not be friend."

"I am like thee, O, Night, cruel and awful; for my bosom is lit by burning ships at sea, and my lips are wet with blood of slain warriors."

"Nay, thou art not like me, O, Madman; for the desire for a sister-spirit is yet upon thee, and thou hast not become a law unto thyself."

"I am like thee, O, Night, joyous and glad; for he who dwells in my shadow is now drunk with virgin wine, and she who follows me is sinning mirthfully."

"Nay, thou art not like me, O, Madman, for thy soul is wrapped in the veil of seven folds and thou holdest not thy heart in thine hand."

"I am like thee, O, Night, patient and passionate; for in my breast a thousand dead lovers are buried in shrouds of withered kisses."

"Yea, Madman, art thou like me? Art thou like me? And canst thou ride the tempest as a steed, and grasp the lightning as a sword?

"Like thee, O, Night, like thee, mighty and high, and my throne is built upon heaps of fallen Gods; and before me too pass the days to kiss the hem of my garment but never to gaze at my face."

"Art thou like me, child of my darkest heart? And dost thou think my untamed thoughts and speak my vast language?"

"Yea, we are twin brothers, O, Night; for thou revealest space and I reveal my soul."

38

Faces

I have seen a face with a thousand countenances, and a face that was but a single countenance as if held in a mould.

I have seen a face whose sheen I could look through to the ugliness beneath, and a face whose sheen I had to lift to see how beautiful it was.

I have seen an old face much lined with nothing, and a smooth face in which all things were graven.

I know faces, because I look through the fabric my own eye weaves, and behold the reality beneath.

I know faces.

39

The Greater Sea

My soul and I went down to the great sea to bathe. And when we reached the shore, we went about looking for a hidden and lonely place. But as we walked, we saw a man sitting on a grey rock taking pinches of salt from a bag and throwing them into the sea.

"This is the pessimist," said my soul, "Let us leave this place. We cannot bathe here."

We walked on until we reached an inlet. There we saw, standing on a white rock, a man holding a bejewelled box, from which he took sugar and threw it into the sea.

"And this is the optimist," said my soul, "And he too must not see our naked bodies."

Further on we walked. And on a beach we saw a man picking up dead fish and tenderly putting them back into the water.

A greater wave.

"And we cannot bathe before him," said my soul. "He is the humane philanthropist." And we passed on.

Then we came where we saw a man tracing his shadow on the sand. Great waves came and erased it. But he went on tracing it again and again. "He is the mystic," said my soul, "Let us leave him."

And we walked on, till in a quiet cove we saw a man scooping up the foam and putting it into an alabaster bowl. "He is the idealist," said my soul, "Surely he must not see our nudity."

And on we walked. Suddenly we heard a voice crying, "This is the sea. This is the deep sea. This is the vast and mighty sea." And when we reached the voice it was a man whose back was turned to the sea, and at his ear he held a shell, listening to its murmur.

And my soul said, "Let us pass on. He is the realist, who turns his back on the whole he cannot grasp, and busies himself with a fragment." So we passed on.

And in a weedy place among the rocks was a man with his head buried in the sand. And I said to my soul, "We can bathe here, for he cannot see us." "Nay," said my soul, "For he is the most deadly of them all. He is the puritan."

Then a great sadness came over the face of my soul, and into her voice. "Let us go hence," she said, "For there is no lonely, hidden place where we can bathe. I would not have this wind lift my golden hair, or bare my white bosom in this air, or let the light disclose my scared nakedness."

Then we left that sea to seek the Greater Sea.

There is none who can be trusted, none to whom one can disclose any secret. The poet and his soul, witnessing these examples, "left that sea to seek the Greater Sea."

40

Crucified

I cried to men, "I would be crucified!" And they said, "Why should your blood be upon our heads?"

And I answered, "How else shall you be exalted except by crucifying madmen?"

And they heeded and I was crucified. And the crucifixion appeased me.

And when I was hanged between earth and heaven they lifted up their heads to see me. And they were exalted, for their heads had never before been lifted.

But as they stood looking up at me one called out, "For what art thou seeking atone?"

And another cried, "In what cause dost thou sacrifice thyself?"

The crucifixion appeased me.

For what cause doth thou sacrifice thyself?

And a third said, "Thinkest thou with this price to buy world glory?"

Then said a fourth, "Behold, how he smiles! Can such pain be forgiven?"

And I answered them all, and said: "Remember only that I smiled. I do not atone—nor sacrifice —nor wish for glory; and I have nothing to forgive. I thirsted—and I besought you to give me my blood to drink. For what is there can quench a madman's thirst but his own blood? I was dumb—and I asked wounds of you for mouths. I was imprisoned on your days and nights—and I sought a door into larger days and nights.

And now I go—as others already crucified have gone. And think not we are weary of crucifixion. For we must be crucified by larger and yet larger men, between greater earths and greater heavens."

41

The Astronomer

In the shadow of the temple my friend and I saw a blind man sitting alone. And my friend said, "Behold the wisest man of our land."

Then I left my friend and approached the blind man and greeted him. And we conversed.

After a while I said, "Forgive my question, but since when hast thou been blind?"

"From my birth," he answered.

Said I, "And what path of wisdom followest thou?"

Said he, "I am an astronomer."

Then he placed his hand upon his breast, saying, "I watch all these suns and moons and stars."

A blind man watched the sun, moon and stars.

42

The Great Longing

Here I sit between my brother the mountain and my
sister the sea. We three are one in loneliness, and the
love that binds us together is deep and strong and strange.
Nay, it is deeper than my sister's depth and stronger than
my brother's strength, and stranger than the strangeness of
my madness. Aeons upon aeons have passed since the first
grey dawn made us visible to one another; and though we
have seen the birth and the fullness and the death of many
worlds, we are still eager and young. We are young and eager and yet we are mateless and unvisited, and though we lie
in unbroken half embrace, we are uncomforted.

And what comfort is there for controlled desire and un-
spent passion? Whence shall come the flaming god to warm my
sister's bed? And what she-torrent shall quench my brother's
fire? And who is the woman that shall command my heart?

In the stillness of the night my sister murmurs in her
sleep the fire-god's unknown name, and my brother calls
afar upon the cool and distant goddess. But upon whom I
call in my sleep I know not.

I do not know that for which I long.

43

Said a Blade of Grass

Said a blade of grass to an autumn leaf, "You make such a noise falling! You scatter all my winter dreams."

Said the leaf indignant, "Low-born and low-dwelling! Songless, peevish thing!

You live not in the upper air and you cannot tell the sound of singing." Then the autumn leaf lay down upon the earth and slept. And when spring came she waked again— and she was a blade of grass.

And when it was autumn and her winter sleep was upon her, and above her through all the air the leaves were falling, she muttered to herself, "O these autumn leaves! They make such a noise! They scatter all my winter dreams."

*You make such a
noise when falling.*

44

The Eye

Said the Eye one day, "I see beyond these valleys a mountain veiled with blue mist. Is it not beautiful?"

The Ear listened, and after listening intently awhile, said, "But where is any mountain? I do not hear."

Then the Hand spoke and said, "I am trying in vain to feel it or touch it, and I can find no mountain."

And the Nose said, "There is no mountain, I cannot smell it." Then the Eye turned the other way, and they all began to talk together about the Eye's strange delusion. And they said, "Something must be the matter with the Eye."

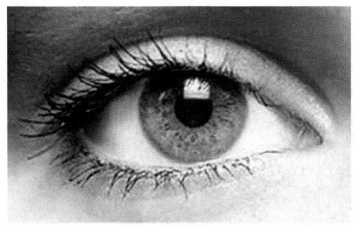

I see a mountain.

45

The Two Learned Men

Once there lived in the ancient city of Afkar two learned men who hated and belittled each other's learning. For one of them denied the existence of the gods and the other was a believer.

One day the two met in the market-place, and amidst their followers they began to dispute and to argue about the existence or the non-existence of the gods. And after hours of contention they parted.

That evening the unbeliever went to the temple and prostrated himself before the altar and prayed the gods to forgive his wayward past.

And the same hour the other learned man, he who had upheld the gods, burned his sacred books. For he had become an unbeliever.

Two learned men argued about the existence of the gods.

46

When My Sorrow Was Born

When my sorrow was born I nursed it with care, and watched over it with loving tenderness.

And my Sorrow grew like all living things, strong and beautiful and full of wondrous delights.

And we loved one another, my Sorrow and I, and we loved the world about us; for Sorrow had a kindly heart and mine was kindly with Sorrow. And when we conversed, my Sorrow and I, our days were winged and our nights were girdled with dreams; for Sorrow had an eloquent tongue, and mine was eloquent with Sorrow.

And when we sang together, my Sorrow and I, our neighbors sat at their windows and listened; for our songs were deep as the sea and our melodies were full of strange memories.

And when we walked together, my Sorrow and I, people gazed at us with gentle

We loved one another, my Sorrow and I.

eyes and whispered in words of exceeding sweetness. And there were those who looked with envy upon us, for Sorrow was a noble thing and I was proud with Sorrow.

But my Sorrow died, like all living things, and alone I am left to muse and ponder.

And now when I speak my words fall heavily upon my ears. And when I sing my songs my neighbours come not to listen. And when I walk the streets no one looks at me.

Only in my sleep I hear voices saying in pity, "See, there lies the man whose Sorrow is dead."

"When My Sorrow Was Born" continues this theme. Sorrow is world-wisdom, insight, and experience, the converse of Love. The poet walks with Sorrow and dreams with Sorrow, his songs "deep as the sea and our melodies ... full of strange memories." Sorrow is kind, strong, elegant, sweet, and noble. But Sorrow died, like all living things, and left the poet alone. Now he goes unnoticed, not listened to, and pitied by others. But "When My Joy Was Born" loudly proclaims the poet's exultation in the marketplace. No one wanted to hear of the joy of another, and so Joy died of isolation.

47

Empathy

Empathy comes from the Greek *empatheia*—*em* (into) and *pathos* (feeling)—a kind of travel into something. The notion is that we enter another person's experience as we might enter another country, to discover its customs, a border crossing by way of query: "What grows where you are? What are the laws? What animals graze there?"

Empathy is not inate; rather, it is a skill to master. Having a sympathetic manner or using a caring tone may be comforting, but it isn't empathy. We must voice the right words to show empathy. Empathy requires that we understand how a person feels specifically, not in the abstract. Doing this takes imagination—to imagine, we must ask questions.

Empathy requires expressing naivety—communicating that you know nothing. And that you are relying upon the person with whom you seek to empathize to help you understand their experience.

Empathy is walking a mile in someone else's shoes; Sympathy is being sorry their feet hurt.

48

And When My Joy Was Born

And when my joy was born I held it in my arms and stood on the house-top shouting, "Come ye, my neighbours, come and see, for Joy this day is born unto me.

Come and behold this gladsome thing that laugheth in the sun." But none of my neighbours came to look upon my Joy, and great was my astonishment.

And every day for seven moons I proclaimed my Joy from the house-top—and yet no one heeded me. And my Joy and I were alone, unsought and unvisited.

Then my Joy grew pale and weary because no other heart but mine held its loveliness and no other lips kissed its lips. Then my Joy died of isolation.

And now I only remember my dead Joy in remembering my dead Sorrow. But memory is an autumn leaf that murmurs in the wind and then is heard no more.

My Joy was born.

49

Conclusion

Gibran studies how the individual functions in society. In "The Perfect World," the poet describes himself as a lost soul, "a human chaos, a nebula of confused elements." In contrast, he sees the world around him as complete and ordered, everything precisely measured, assigned, and accurate. Everything from eating, sleeping, working, playing, thinking, feeling, going about one's daily routines—all is perfectly measured and prescribed.

Of course, the world is not perfect when we look beneath the masks of daily life. Still, the perceptions of the outcast, the stranger, the madman, stand in stark contrast to that inner layer of people's motives: hypocrisy, greed, pride, sloth, ambition, vanity, conformity. These people do not really see anything wrong with the ways of the world. In "War," justice is literally so blind that it would punish all to make suffering equal.

It is a perfect world, a world of consummate excellence, a world of supreme wonders, the ripest fruit in God's garden, the master-thought of the universe. But why should I be here, O God, I, a green seed of unfulfilled passion, a mad tempest that seeketh neither east nor west, a bewildered fragment from a burnt planet? Why am I here, O God of lost souls, thou who art lost amongst the gods?

Kahlil Gibran's writings are a unique synthesis of creative figures hovering on the edge of society. He constructed the madman and the solitary as a figure of sagacity and reflectiveness, one who ultimately no longer needs to rebel because he has learned how to disengage, to keep a right distance while nevertheless relating to others with compassion and kindness.

Thus did the figure of the madman come to be universalized for those who had blossomed with the original fruit of Gibran's insight.

Because of this fervent opposition to demands to conform Gibran often found himself at odds with the established institutions. He admired the brave souls and mighty minds who challenged societal restrictions and limitations.

Gibran was fascinated by creative figures hovering on the edge of society.

Gibran called his little apartment and studio in New York City "The Hermitage," where he hosted writers and artists like himself in ethnic origin and sharing a common set of values. But Gibran's unique world-view and his combination of creative forces, is a great cultural treasure. His writings, while standing on their own, are an important resource for reflecting on the themes of solitude, society, and self.

RONIN
Books-for-Independent-Minds

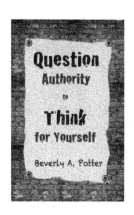

Visit *roninpub. com* to see our books, then use isbn to order in Ronin's store or ANY bookstore - and Enjoy!

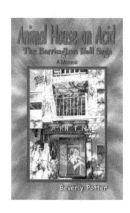

Bookstores: Order from PGW/Ingram

Printed in the USA
CPSIA information can be obtained
at www.ICGtesting.com
JSHW012013140824
68134JS00024B/2394